TELL ME A SWISS JOKE!

4⁰⁰ —
Human
1/20

TELL ME A SWISS JOKE!

Humor from Switzerland
Believe it or not, it exists!

Collected and edited by René Hildbrand
Translated by Birgit Rommel

Benteli Publishers Berne

© 1987 by Benteli Publishers, Berne
Layout by Benteliteam
Typesetting and printing by Benteli Inc., Berne
Printed in Switzerland
ISBN 3-7165-0582-X

"William Tell is still the only Swiss
the whole world knows."
Friedrich Dürrenmatt

Foreword

Switzerland is small, has tall mountains, is situated in the middle of Western Europe, comprises four distinct cultural areas, and has an eccentric form of government. This variety in culture and idiom is a typical feature of Switzerland and the Swiss; and their humor is just as colourful and varied. That is why there is no such thing as *the* Swiss joke.

It is claimed that the Swiss have no sense of humor, which does not amuse us at all... Admittedly, a ready wit is not what the Swiss are most commonly known for: They have no peers in such fields as watchmaking, chocolate production, or banking; and even as the traditional owners of the longest-lasting neutrality and the highest mountains they are not free-and-easy with their laughter. Yet many Swiss have a highly developed sense of humor, and some seem to believe they are humor incarnate — and who am I to question that!

Seriously, though, even if the Swiss often do not laugh until they have had time to think, their laughter, when it comes, comes from the heart. And, like love, humor and laughter must come from the heart.

The Swiss — whose souls, incidentally, still soar to alpine heights — are averse to being labelled money-grubbers. But if all the world loves the Swiss franc, why shouldn't we?

Even if you know the world, that doesn't mean you know Switzerland. I hope that in this small collection of jokes and humor I have managed to capture some of the characteristics, virtues, and vices of this enviable nation.

René Hildbrand

Humor
set out from
Switzerland to go and
look at the world.
Unfortunately,
it hasn't come back
from its travels yet...!

"So you've just been on holiday in Switzerland,"
one Englishman said to another.
"What did you think of the Matterhorn?"
"You should know better than to ask,"
was the reply.
"You know I'm not at all musical."

**On putting down the morning paper
a Swiss citizen sighed:
"Everything is tried out
on mice first, except politicians,
those they try out on people."**

A psychiatrist tried to reassure a Swiss politician
during a therapy session:
"Utter rubbish! The whole world is not
against you. The whole of Switzerland, perhaps,
but not the whole world!"

An example of Swiss hospitality
in the private sphere:
"Come by for coffee after Sunday lunch,
then you'll be sure to be home
in time for dinner."

Heard on an American TV show:
"Switzerland has finally decided to give up its
legendary neutrality. She has declared that
after the next war she'll back the victor."

Looking out of the window in the morning
has been banned for Swiss civil servants:
otherwise, what would be left for them
to do in the afternoons?

> *A Swiss prayer:*
> *"God, give me patience,*
> *but quickly!"*

During the second world war,
the Germans are said to have sent a letter to the
Swiss government asking whether they were
in a position to supply tanks.
The Federal government replied:
"Can you manage with two,
or do you need all three?"

What fairy tale does a Swiss
enjoy most?
His income tax returns.

When God had finished creating Switzerland
in outline, he said to the first Swiss:
"I shall grant you three wishes.
What would you like?"
"Well, first of all, imposing mountains."
And the Lord created the most
magnificent mountains.
"What else? No need to be shy."
"Green, juicy meadows with cows on them that
will produce a lot of excellent milk."
And God created green meadows with excellent
dairy cattle. The Swiss decided to make sure,
milked one of the cows, and tasted the milk.
"Is it good?" God asked in a friendly way.
"Excellent! Taste it Yourself, Lord!" and he
passed God a glass of milk.
"You're right, it is excellent", God said.
"And what would you like now?"
"Three francs for the glass of milk!"
the Swiss replied.

A popular Swiss motto:
"Money may not make you happy, but it does make you rich."

Zurich

The British journalist Willi Frischauer once said:
"Zurich is the most boring city in Europe."
Another foreigner said: "Zurich?
A yell! I literally yawned tears!"
When Erich Kästner, the author, was staying
in Zurich, he said to a Swiss colleague
one night at about midnight:
"Well, I think I'd better go to bed now.
Where else is there to go in Zurich?"
And in a visitor's book it says:
"Zurich: before twelve a nice city,
after twelfe a pity."
A Viennese introduced a nice macabre touch:
"Zurich is only half as big as Vienna's
central cemetry, but it is twice as boring."
Yet another comment on Switzerland's
largest city: "It is good to be born in Zurich,
and it is a worthy place to die in;
but what does one do in between?"

A keen huntsman from the Grisons arrived home
at 4 a. m. from a somewhat alcoholic reunion
with fellow sportsmen.
In order not to wake his wife, he got undressed
very quietly. She woke up all the same and, still
half asleep (and thinking he was getting dressed),
asked: "Where are you going?"
With great presence of mind he replied:
"Hunting!"
A little more awake, she said: "But it's raining."
"Raining, is it? Well, then I'll stay at home!"
He finished undressing, got into bed,
and went peacefully to sleep.

A Swiss who had come into money said:
"At last I can afford champagne and caviar.
All I've got to do now is learn to like them!"

I recently started a trading agency, but am not yet quite clear on the profit margins I should achieve. When is a deal really a deal?

When you can prove to the tax inspector
that it wasn't one!

> **She: "Why do you want me to hold your earlobes when we kiss?"**
> **He: "I once lost my wallet while kissing!"**

A Swiss to a German: "And may our common
language continue to be the only bond
that separates us!"

A Swiss was asked whether he believed in heredity:
"Of course, at least that's how I came by my money!"

*What is the difference between prosperity
and recession?
As I'm financially and professionally well off,
I can't quite put my finger on the definition.*

Prosperity is: caviar, Rolls, and girl friend.
Recession is: chicken, trains, and mother!

The shortest book in the world:
"A history of Swiss humor!"

If you forget about the mountains and lakes,
Switzerland is the same as anywhere else.

What's the difference between a Swiss bank
and a casino?
???
In the casino they have
one-armed bandits!

**The cannibals
took a Swiss they had caught
to their headman.
He checked the identity papers
and said:
"Let him go. He's from Zurich,
his lead content will be far too high!"**

*Why do so many Swiss banks have bars
on their windows?
That's simple, it's to help the bank directors
get used to the idea of them.*

In a Swiss resort
the violinist from the small orchestra
in the dining room went over
to one of the tables.
"Excuse me, were you the gentleman
who asked for some Mozart?"
"Certainly not," was the reply, "I asked for some
roast veal!"

**There are numerous jokes on the lack of
height of the people from canton Appenzell.
For example:
People from Appenzell have no fleas.
But fleas might well have Appenzellers.
Question: Why are there so many small
Appenzellers, and so few tall ones?
Answer: The small ones are the result of
domestic relations and the tall ones
of foreign relations.**

A Swiss banker
is a man
who rents out
umbrellas
when the sun
is shining and
demands their return
when it rains.

A Zurich broker:
"Swiss shareholders are lambs
when business is good,
tigers when it's bad –
but they're beasts
all of the time!"

*I run an exclusive fashion boutique and have
a very odd question. One of my regular customers
who spends quite a lot in my shop always pays
with damp banknotes. What do you think
might be behind that?*

Probably your customer's husband weeps
as he hands her the money...

A young Swiss, on receiving notice from
his draft board to report for induction into
the armed services, managed to convince
the board officer that he was half blind.
That evening the youth went to the cinema.
When the lights came on he noticed that
a member of the draft board was sitting next
to him. Not in the least embarrassed, the youth
tapped him on the shoulder and asked:
"Excuse me, madam, this is the train
for Berne, isn't it?"

*A Swiss jeweler was on the point of death,
and the priest passed him a silver cross.
The dying man weighed it in his hand.
"I can't give you more than ten francs for it,"
were his dying words.*

A boy who was
repeatedly beaten
at home
declared:
"I'm going to try
and find a job with the
Swiss national football team;
they never beat
anyone!"

*Switzerland
is the only country
where the mountains
are higher
than the taxes.*

March 21st is an important date
in the Federal Parliament:
It marks the end of winter hibernation
and the beginning of springtime lethargy.

Guest to waiter:
"This really is not good enough!"
"What isn't, sir?"
"The fly in my soup is cold!"

Seen in the 'Personal Column' of a Swiss paper:
"Attractive blonde (25) would like to marry
a man who can kiss just like a footballer
after a goal has been scored.
Preferably a forward."

Herr Huber asked for the menu.
On noting the juicy prices he said to his wife:
"Well, my little dumpling,
what would you like to eat?»

Typically Swiss: "I'm glad I bumped into you,
Huber. Can you lend me a hundred francs?"
"Sorry, I haven't a cent on me."
"And at home?"
"Thanks for asking, they're all fine!"

Someone called Swissair to ask: "How long
does a flight take from Zurich to Tokyo?"
The telephonist under stress replied:
"Just a moment."
"Thank you for the information,"
the caller said, and hung up.

Note behind a wind-screen wiper:
"Dear officer, I'm just taking my grandmother
some cakes and wine. It also appears that
someone has stolen one of my sparking plugs.
Should my car be in a no-parking area,
may I ask you to overlook this —
shall be back in no time!"

I love telling jokes.
But whenever I really get started
my wife picks up her knitting.
Why would she do that?

Probably because your jokes are so old that she
needs to keep her hands busy to avoid
strangling you ...!

I'm really fed up.
Our neighbour's cow
always grazes
on our meadow.
What should I do?

Stop complaining and
start milking!

A young lady called up the sports section
of a paper:
"When did the Basle football club
win its last match?"
After a long wait she was told: "May 17th."
"Thank you, now I can work out
when the baby's due!"

A wife to her husband who was watching
a match between Switzerland and Italy on TV:
"Darling, I'm going to climb up this ladder now
because I want to paint the ceiling.
If I should fall down, would you please call
an ambulance at half-time?"

A guest shouted at the waiter:
"Do you call this strong coffee?"
"Certainly, sir. You've only taken one sip
and you're already shouting!"

*Why do the English
drink so much tea?*
Try their coffee!

"You always win at cards, and never
on the horses."
"You try keeping a horse up your sleeve..."

**A lorry
travelling from France
to Switzerland was stopped
at the Swiss border.
"Customs check! What are you
carrying?"
"Tousands of oysters."
"All right. Open them up!"**

I've heard that this year
we're in for
a very long winter.
Is that true?

It won't be that bad.
Remember,
we already had
half of it in the
summer.

During the second world war, American bombers accidentally flew over Swiss territory. The Swiss Army reacted with Hunters and artillery. Apparently a Swiss anti-aircraft unit radioed this warning to a US bomber: "You are now over Swiss territory." The American reply was "We know." When the Swiss started shooting, the American bomber crew radioed back: "You're off target." The Swiss reply: "We know."

Boss: "You're 30 minutes late
every morning."
Clerk: "I know, but then I leave
30 minutes earlier every evening."

In a Swiss school,
the teacher
asked one of the pupils:
"Who was the first man?"
"William Tell."
"No, really, Adam was
the first man."
"Well, if you're going to include
foreigners..."

Is there any life on Mars?

No, out of the question, otherwise the Swiss would have sent a diplomat there ages ago.

"What was the name of that hotel in Lugano that we liked so much?"
"I can't remember for the moment. Let me just go and check it on the cutlery."

Doctor: "What sports do you do?"
Patient: "Swimming, fencing, tennis, and boxing."
Doctor: "Since when?"
Patient: "I'm starting the day after tomorrow."

Two Swiss lawyers were sitting in a restaurant
talking shop. One of them called across
to a waiter and asked:
"Does anyone here have a copy of the
Swiss criminal code by any chance?"
The owner immediately went up to the table,
his face scarlet:
"Of course I'll take the wine back, gentlemen..."

**Max got home very late.
"Where have you been?
The downstairs clock has just struck four,"
his wife mumbled from the bed.
Max: "Go back to sleep, darling.
The clock was about to strike midnight,
and I stopped it at the fourth chime
so that it wouldn't wake you up."**

*Recently my boss told me that I was the only one
on his staff who could not be replaced
by a computer. What can he mean?*

Perhaps he meant that so far
they've not invented a machine that does
absolutely nothing!

**A Swiss politician: "I started with nothing.
All I had was my brains."**

*I recently served a five-month prison sentence.
Through some error they kept me inside
for an additional week.
What can I do?*

Have them deduct it next time...

"Snails are our speciality", the head waiter of a Bernese restaurant informed the guest. "I know, I was served by one yesterday!"

A national councilor
started his speech
like this:
"Before I speak to you I should like to
tell you something!"

Toni took the train from Zurich to Berne.
He had no ticket.
His excuse when asked to show it:
"They'd sold out of tickets in Zurich!"

"Waiter, there's a fly in my soup!"
"Not for long, sir. Look at the spider
sitting on the rim of the plate!"

41

> *"Are you enjoying your steak?"*
> *"Very much, only the price*
> *is unpalatable!"*

In future, Swiss football players will have to pay
their barbers 30% more. The reason:
The barbers want more for shaving
such long faces.

Policeman: "Why did you ignore
three successive red lights?"
Driver: "I never stop for red.
I'm a capitalist!"

I'm a bank manager.
Yesterday our cleaner asked me
for the key to the strongroom.
What could that mean?

Perhaps it's too much of a bother for her
to open it with a hairpin
whenever it needs to be cleaned!

**Do you know the difference
between jogging and sex?
???
No? Then you'd better keep
jogging!**

*In a restaurant:
"Waiter, this soup
tastes funny."
"Then why aren't you
laughing?"*

A Swiss was complaining about the whole
family constantly watching television:
"My daughters never miss any of the films, so
they don't do their homework. My wife would
much rather watch 'Dallas' or 'Dynasty' than get
on with her housework. I swear that as soon as
the World Cup is over I'll unplug the set!"

**Swiss diplomats are people who must be able
to keep silent in at least four languages.**

*A guest exclaimed enthusiastically:
"This pattern on the butter is charming!"
The waiter, proudly: "Isn't it. I did it
with my comb."*

A seventeen-year-old was inadvertently stopped
in a traffic check in Zurich.
"Where's your driving license?"
the policeman asked.
"I had always assumed you didn't get one
until you were eighteen," the youth answered
in embarrassment.

At an athletics meeting just before the
javelin event, Willi said to a friend:
"I really must concentrate now.
My mother-in-law is over there watching."
His friend asked:
"Do you honestly think you can hit her?"

A young couple was sitting
dreamily on a park bench.
She breathed:
"Darling, tell me something
exciting."
"Sure", he whispered back,
"FC Zurich lost three nil."

Why do Swiss politicians seldom laugh? Because they don't want to be accused of living only for pleasure.

A football star was asked
how he accounted for the fact
that he earned much more
than the president of the Swiss national bank.
His reply: "Simple, I'm much better at football
than the president of the
Swiss national bank."

A Swiss hotel has hung up a notice
behind its reception desk:
"We hope you'll really feel at home here —
just don't behave as if you were!"

I'm 62 and in love with a 20-year-old.
Despite my millions, she refuses to marry me.
What can I do?

Tell her you're 80!

Two men were standing
next to each other at a bar.
One was still sober, the other already fairly tipsy.
The tipsy one swayed towards
the sober one and said:
"You'll have to go easy on the drinking,
you know. Your face is already quite blurred."

Last night my wife told me
she doesn't want to see me any more.
I was desperate.
What would you have done?

Switched the light off!

A trainer said to the Swiss boxer, Sepp Iten:
"If you keep on boxing like this, you'll qualify
for this year's Nobel peace prize."

The vicar was disappointed:
"This is unbelievable. No-one in church,
not even the organist. Who's going to play?"
"Brazil against Mexico!"

*I've a passion for flying, and I can
even afford it.
Can you advise me on the best way
to acquire a Swiss army plane?*

That's easy! Buy a plot of land,
and wait!

She: "Darling, what would life be without me!?" He: "Cheaper, darling, much cheaper..."

**In future, all football internationals
in which the Swiss national team is playing
will start in the early afternoon.
The reason: Coffee and cakes
are served at 4 p.m.
in the old people's home.**

"What's for dinner today?" a recently married
man asked on returning from work.
"I don't know, darling,
the label has come off the can!"

**Guest to waiter:
"What would you recommend
to round off this meal?"
"A generous tip, sir!"**

Although I read about the danger of
smoking almost daily, I simply can't give it up.
What's your advice?

Give up reading!

**What happens if a woman and two men are
marooned on a desert island?
If they're Spanish, one of the men
will kill the other.
If they're Italian, the woman will kill
one of the two men.
If they're British, nothing will happen because
there'll be no-one to introduce
the two men to each other.
If they're Swiss, nothing will happen either,
because the men will be talking shop.
If they're French, there won't be any problem.**

Swiss television
has decided to show
no more slow motion shots
of the Swiss national
football team.
The reason:
They are slow enough
already.

What's the quickest way
of making a small fortune
in Switzerland?

By giving an investment counselor
a large fortune to work with…

Trudi crossed the road while the lights were red
and walked straight into the arms of a
policeman on the other side.
He asked:
"Are you color-blind?"
"No, but when the lights are green there's always
such a crush on the crossing!"

**A national councilor was involved in a traffic
accident and was taken to hospital.
A few days later he received a card
from his fellow parliamentarians. It read:
"Here are the results of our vote
on the motion that you get well soon:
170 yes, 30 no, 10 abstentions.
Best wishes, your colleagues."**

*For eleven years now our son has been studying
at various British universities.
We are a little worried about his future.
Have you any idea how old our son will be
when he finally graduates?*

I hate to say so, but he'll be old...!

**"You never think about anything but
football!" Silvia complained. "I bet you can't
even remember when we got married."
"Of course I remember, it was on the day
Switzerland drew against Germany."**

In a letter to her son,
a Swiss mother added a PS.
"I had meant to enclose
a hundred francs,
but stupidly I'd already
sealed the envelope."

If we had no federal councilors in Switzerland, we wouldn't have so much to laugh about.

Text seen at an inn:
Don't get divorced simply because
your wife can't cook.
Eat here and keep your wife
as a hobby!

Instead of keeping to 25 mph in town,
Fritz was driving at 50 mph
and was promptly stopped for speeding.
His excuse: "My gas tank was on empty,
and I tought I had to get to the next gas station
as quickly as possible!"

I find rail travel far too expensive.
Isn't there anything cheaper
than a second class ticket?

Certainly! All you need is four legs and a tail!

There seems to be something wrong with my car.
Whenever I'm doing more than 100 mph
there's a knocking noise from the engine.
What could it be?

Probably your guardian angel!

Anita, a secretary, got back late to the office
after lunch. She explained to her boss:
"I burnt my lunch, and there was so much
smoke that I couldn't see the kitchen clock."

A guest complained that his steak was tough.
The chef retorted:
"I was grilling steaks before you had started
cutting teeth!"
"And why did you wait so long
before serving them?"

*How can you
make more
out of a franc?*

Drill four holes
and sell it
as a button!

We are about to celebrate our 30th wedding anniversary. My wife is a wine lover. What region and vintage would you recommend for such an occasion?

Hard to say. Do you want to celebrate or forget?

Two Swiss politicians were flying over
their country in a helicopter. They were trying
to decide what they could do to please
the Swiss population.
"Let's drop a 100 franc note," one of them said,
"then at least one citizen will be pleased."
The other politician had a better idea:
"Let's drop ten 10 franc notes,
then ten citizens will be pleased."
The pilot had the best idea:
"If I drop both of you,
then six million Swiss citizens will be pleased!"

*We're paying Fr. 1400 a month for our
two-bedroom flat, and the kitchen is tiny.
What's your reaction?*

That doesn't sound so bad!
After all, if you're paying so much rent,
you can hardly afford to cook a great deal...!

**Overheard at a job centre:
"How many jobs have you had
in the past year?"
"Four."
"Do you do casual work?"
"No, I'm a football trainer."**

A bored wife looking at the TV set:
"Still playing football? I thought they declared
the Swiss cup winner last year."

"Boxing is a
wonderful sport."
"Really? Are you
a boxer?"
"No, a dentist."

I am 55 years old, but feel considerably older.
Is there any way I can qualify for
old-age pension payments before I am 65?

Yes! Throw away your passport and
have yourself assessed...!

"In other words, doctor,
you're calling me an alcoholic?"
"No, not quite that. Let me put it like this:
If I were a bottle of whisky, I shouldn't want
to be left alone with you in a room."

Why are two fried eggs more expensive in a
restaurant than two scrambled eggs?

Probably because you can count fried eggs!

**A reporter asked a football trainer:
"How can your team manage to win
every match?"
"I don't understand it, either. What's more,
before every game I bet the referee
five thousand francs that we'll lose."**

It's better to have wet feet
than a dry throat.

*I'm having an operation next week.
They tell me it will cost a thousand francs.
Do you think it might be dangerous?*

There's no need to worry.
Nowadays you can't get a dangerous operation
for only a thousand francs.

> *Are there still people around who don't believe in the pill?*
>
> Yes, they're usually called fathers!

A drunk was trying to open a lamp-post with his latch-key. In passing, a policeman muttered: "It's unlikely that there'll be anyone at home." "Of course there is," the drunk replied, "there's a light on upstairs."

"Hello, is that Alcoholics Anonymous?"
"Yes."
"Good, then you'll be able to tell me whether I should serve white or red wine with my roast duck."

A Swiss politician abroad: "They always say the Swiss have no sense of humor. We don't think that's funny at all."

> # What is a trio?
> The Moscow Symphony Orchestra after its return from a concert tour of Switzerland.

A neighbour: "You had a real family row yesterday evening, didn't you?"
"Nonsense, my husband was simply arguing with the referee during a football match on TV."

What would be the very first thing you'd do if I were to give you a hundred francs, just like that?

I'd count them!

Why is there always such a crush at stadium exits
after a football match?
Is there no way to avoid that?

There is. If everyone were to remain seated
until the others had left,
there would never be any trouble!

An excuse for being late for school:
"Our cock died, and so the whole village
overslept."

A boxer's wife is awakened
in the middle of the night.
She can just make out a burglar in the darkness.
She prods her husband and whispers:
"Wake up, Fritz, someone wants
a private training session."

> *Guest: "Waiter,*
> *a toothpick, please!"*
> *Waiter: "Yes sir, there'll be one free*
> *any moment!"*

I'm a sixteen-year-old girl,
and my greatest wish is to own a villa,
drive a big car, have six children
and a super husband.
How should I set about getting them?

I'd advise you to get the order right first!

"Werner knows a lot about football."
"Does he know all the rules?"
"No, but he knows the nationalities of all
the players in Swiss first division football."

"How would you like your tea, with or without rum?" "Normally I drink it with rum, but without tea."

"Just imagine, one of our club members
topped six meters in the pole vault!"
"That's fantastic."
"Yes and no. He was disqualified."
"Why?"
"He forgot his pole..."

**Toni was somewhat tipsy when he got home.
"Frieda," he called to his wife in the bedroom,
"start nagging, else I won't be able to find my
bed!"**

*What will I get if I invest one million francs
at three percent?*

You'll get a reputation for being
a complete idiot!

Franz was late for work and told his boss:
"I found a one thousand franc note."
"I see, and there was such a long queue
at the lost property office?"
"No, but I had to stand on it for ages
before it was safe to pick it up."

Fourteen goals were scored against a Swiss
football club in three games. The club president
made the goalkeeper the following offer:
"We'll sign a contract for Fr. 100,000 a month —
if you move to another club!"

I read somewhere that a third of what we eat
would be quite enough to live on.
What happens to the other two thirds?

That's what the doctors live on!

Three generals were discussing courage.
The Russian general ordered one of his soldiers
to give a demonstration:
"Climb up this telephone pole
and jump straight down!"
The soldier obeyed the command and was
carried off by the medical orderlies.
"There you are, gentlemen, that's courage!"
The American general gave one of his soldiers
this command:
"Climb up this telephone pole
and jump down backwards!"
The soldier did, and was also carried off
by medical orderlies.
"There you are, gentlemen, that's courage!"
The Swiss commander of the general staff
gave his command:
"Climb up the same pole, turn a double somersault,
and jump down!"
The soldier shook his head:
"Sir, you must be mad, sir!"
The Swiss commander:
"There you are, gentlemen, that's courage!"

At half-time,
the trainer of the
Swiss national football team
went up to the radio commentator:
"Do please speak a little slower.
My boys can't keep up with you."

At midday, a somewhat inebriated
national councilor phoned the reception desk
of the Bellevue hotel in Berne:
"Ex — excuse me, ca — can you tell me
when the hotel bar opens?"
"At five o'clock!" the receptionist replied.
Two hours later the councilor,
now thoroughly drunk, phoned again:
"Ex — excuse me, when does the bar open?"
The receptionist: "At five o'clock,
which is what I told you at midday!"
The MP did not appear to have understood.
At three o'clock the phone rang again.
The same man was at the other end —
he could hardly speak:
"I — I really must — must know w — when
the hotel bar opens!"
The receptionist lost her cool: "I've already
told you twice that it opens at five o'clock.
But it's most unlikely that in your condition
they'll let you in!"
"I don't want to be let in, I want to be let out..."

After a meal in a restaurant,
cups of brownish liquid were served.
Fritz took a sip and
pushed his cup away in disgust.
The waiter bent over him helpfully:
"Can I get you something else, sir?"
"Please. If this is coffee, bring me tea,
and if it's tea, then I'd like a coffee."

A sports journalist was reading the sports results
on Swiss television. In one report he suddenly
started to stutter as he read off what it said
in his manuscript:
"O ... O ... O ... O ... O ..."
In agitation the producer whispered:
"Do go on, they're only the Olympic rings!"

Franz
asked his boss for
three days off.
"A friend of mine
is getting married
and she wants me to be
the groom."

> *Is it unlucky to postpone your wedding?*
>
> Not if it's for good!

Our best friend is called "Bari",
a beautiful St. Bernard.
We are utterly miserable because
four days ago Bari disappeared.
What are we to do?
Do you think it's worth
putting a lost notice in the paper?

That won't get you very far.
After all, your Bari can't read, can he?

An extraordinarily corpulent man was sitting
in the most expensive restaurant in town.
A friend of his, whom he had not seen for some
considerable time, came up to his table.
"Well, how are things?" he asked.
"Not good at all. The strong franc
is bad for business," the fat man sighed.
"Not good?" his friend repeated. "It doesn't
show, you know. Here you are, eating lobster
and drinking the best wine. It really looks
as if things are going very well indeed."
"You're wrong, my friend," the fat man grunted,
"in the old days I could afford
to bring my wife along!"

Waiter: "Sorry, sir, this table is reserved."
Guest: "That's all right,
just bring me another one!"

Willi
got home late,
and his wife asked:
"What excuse do you have
this time?"
"None!"
"Oh? And you expect me
to believe that?"

"Last Sunday I saw
Beethoven in the Löwen hotel.
What do you say to that?"
"Impossible! The Löwen
is closed on Sundays."

A magician shouted at the night waiter
in a hotel at four in the morning:
"If you don't get me a bottle of whisky
immediately, I'll beat you black and blue!"
At the same time a mouse
peeped out from his cuff and added:
"And that goes for your cat, too!"

The Swiss army
is not particularly popular in canton Ticino.
The Germans don't like having a foreign army
on their territory...

*We are German, and for years we have been
unlucky with our holidays in Switzerland.
Does it really always rain there?*

No, in winter it snows!

**Thommy explained to his teacher:
"I'm sorry, sir, I've only managed twenty lines
of 'I must keep quiet'. My pen squeaked
so much while I was writing that my father
shouted 'can't you keep quiet'!"**

The advocate demanded:
"And why did you throw
your husband out of a moving car,
Frau Müller?"
"What else could I have done,
it was a no-stopping area!"

The Swiss football team
was playing Germany.
In the second half of the match
the Germans confused
a penalty whistle
with the final whistle,
and went home.
Half an hour later
the Swiss scored
their first goal.

How would you define a gentleman?

A gentleman is a man who protects a woman
until he is alone with her!

Karl had an excuse ready when he was stopped
by the police for jumping a red light:
"A huge furniture van with a trailer
crossed the lights ahead of me
and the suction was so strong
that I was literally pulled across!"

*I was recently found guilty in court.
My sentence offers me a choice between
three weeks imprisonment and Fr. 2000.
What shall I do?*

I'd take the money.

What are the main qualifications for the perfect
Swiss civil servant?

He must wear a dark suit and hold his tongue.

The Tour de Suisse cyclists
were sprinting through a village.
One of the spectators said to another:
"Look, the one in the lead is wearing a tie."
"That's no tie, that's his tongue!"

Can you tell me how long cows
have to be milked?

Just like short ones, I should think!

It's better
to eat too much
than to drink
too little.

When was the Swiss army first officially mentioned?

I believe it was in the Bible.
It says there:
"They wore strange garments
and wandered about
in confusion!"

The French president was on a visit
to Switzerland.
Several federal councilors accompanied
their guest in a special train
travelling across the country.
"We're now doing 85 mph!" the Swiss
transport minister said with pride.
The French president replied dryly:
"We have the same problem in France. The trains
are always having to slow down because of
all these construction sites!"

Over the last twenty years the Swiss army
has lost dozens of aircraft in aviation accidents.
And yet they still claim that Switzerland
is not contributing to disarmament.

She: "You used to be happy
if you could see me
for just a few minutes a day."
He: "But that's still true."

*Yesterday my wife said it was incredible
what three whiskies could do to me.
And I hadn't drunk anything at all.*

Perhaps your wife had.

*In a good marriage
no-one wears the pants.*

"Tell me,
how many beers
do you down
during the course of a day?"
"Between ten and twenty."
"Goodness, I couldn't even drink
that much water."
"Nor could I."